★★★ DISCOVERIN

9/11
Courage and Tributes

By **Kristie Kiernan Bouryal**

Illustrated by **Gabe** and **Haruka Ostley**

Designed by James Johnson
www.jamesjohnson.net

Copyedited by RSH Communications

ISBN 978-1-73-299135-4

This book is dedicated to those who fell on September 11, 2001 and those who had to carry on. May America never forget.

Chapter 1

It was a sunny Friday afternoon. The school bell rang, marking the end of the school day. Cousins Tyler, Olivia and Sophia had been waiting for this moment all week. They had plans to spend the weekend at Grandma and Grandpa's house. The family was looking forward to visiting very special tributes created to remember and honor the people who lost their lives on September 11, 2001.

Tyler raced home from school to finish getting his things together for the weekend. At their house, Olivia and Sophia had their bags packed and ready to go. They grabbed their things and were quickly on their way.

At Grandma and Grandpa's house, Grandma was preparing snacks in the kitchen while Grandpa looked out the window, waiting for the kids to arrive. He saw Tyler walking up the front steps and opened the door for him. "Hey, Grandpa," Tyler said as he gave him a big hug. "Hi, T," said Grandpa as he hugged him and helped with his bag. "Are Olivia and Sophia here yet?" Tyler asked. "No," Grandpa replied. "They should be here any minute." Tyler walked in the kitchen to kiss Grandma hello and tell her about his day.

Minutes later, the doorbell rang and the front door flew open. Olivia and Sophia ran in smiling and shouting, "We're here!" They hugged everyone and Grandma asked if the kids were hungry. "Oh, yes," said Olivia as everyone nodded and sat at the table to eat the yummy snacks Grandma prepared.

"OK, so I have been thinking about this all week," said Tyler. "What are the places like that we are going to visit? What can you tell us because I have no idea what to expect?" "I know! I had the same questions!" exclaimed Olivia as she giggled and bit into a chocolate covered strawberry.

Grandma paused and then said, "Well, all of the places you'll see were created to remember and honor people we lost that day, but they are all different and special in their own way."

"Different how?" asked Sophia. "They all have different appearances and even represent different people in some cases," Grandma said. "One is larger while others are smaller, one may focus on first responders while others focus on them plus the people who were just going about their day. But no matter the look or the size or who it represents, I know for certain that you will be very touched by these remembrances."

"I really don't think I can wait anymore! Can we please go now Grandma and Grandpa?" Olivia yelled. "Yes, please can we go now?" asked Sophia as Tyler nodded his head.

Grandma and Grandpa looked at each other and smiled. "What if we go to the one closest to here? We could go and still make it home in time for dinner," said Grandma. "Sure. That's a great idea," Grandpa replied.

"Yes!" the kids exclaimed as they put their dishes in the dishwasher and raced to the bathroom to wash their

hands. Grandma got everyone's coats out of the closet and one by one, they put them on.

After the family fastened their seatbelts, Grandpa began to slowly back the car out of the driveway.

"Do you remember what Grandma and I shared with you about September 11, 2001?" asked Grandpa. "You said it was America's darkest day. Our country was attacked in multiple cities," Tyler replied. "That's right," said Grandpa. "It was a day when the unthinkable happened. Nearly 3,000 people lost their lives. In Shanksville, Pennsylvania, Washington, D.C. and here in New York City, where the famous and tall Twin Towers, which were part of the set of buildings known as the World Trade Center, collapsed."

"That day left many people in this country, and around the world, feeling completely shocked, devastated and deeply saddened," Grandma added. "Each special place we are going to take you to reminds us of the people we lost that day."

"What's the name of the place we are going to now?" asked Tyler. "It's called Angels' Circle and it's right here in Staten Island, New York," Grandma replied.

"How did it get started?" asked Olivia. "It all started thanks to the passion of a special woman named Wendy

Furtado Pellegrino," Grandma replied. "The night of September 11th, Wendy was very upset about what happened," Grandma continued. "She couldn't sleep and was tossing and turning in her bed. She decided to get up, go in her garage and paint a sign that said 'God Bless Our Heroes.' When she finished it, she placed it with candles in the dirt of an empty piece of land right across the street from where she lived."

"What happened next?" asked Sophia. "People responded by placing photos there of people who were missing. As time passed, people started giving Wendy small mass cards from funerals and memorials with photos of the fallen so she could display them on that land," Grandma replied. "Soon, her mailbox was overflowing with images people left for her to add to the remembrance."

"Wendy received an outpouring of support, at the beginning and through the years, from families who lost loved ones, everyday people, politicians and businesses," Grandma said. "For many years now, a local garden center owner, Fred Ariemma, and his sons, Michael and Anthony, have donated plants, flowers, trees, and pavers and they maintain the land."

"That is so kind," Tyler commented. "It really is," said

Grandma. "People donated fencing, had electricity installed so the area could be lit at night and donated money for holiday decorations. People also help her decorate for the holidays. You see, her efforts inspired a lot of people through the years. Together, they all made Angels' Circle as special as it is today," Grandma said.

"The land is at the intersection of two busy roadways and now everyone knows that special place as Angels' Circle," Grandma continued. "All these years later, families and friends still visit regularly, along with tour buses and people from around the world, who want to pay their respects. Wendy also has a memorial service there every year, the night before September 11th."

Tyler, Olivia and Sophia were stunned. "That is an awesome story. I can't wait to see it," said Olivia. "It's incredible that it all started with a sign she painted and put in the dirt," added Tyler. "It is," said Grandma.

Just then, Grandpa made a right-hand turn and pulled into a parking space on the side of the road. "We're here," Grandpa said as Tyler, Olivia and Sophia looked out the window at statues of angels and the American flag flying overhead.

Chapter 2

The family exited the car and held hands to cross the street. As they approached the entrance, a big, black and white sign captured their attention. "Angels' Circle. A circle of love. A landing zone for our angels of September 11, 2001," Tyler read aloud as the family paused before entering.

Inside the fence, the family saw rows and rows of photos of people. "Wow! I can see their faces and names," Olivia said in amazement. Looking down near the front entrance, Sophia noticed several firefighters. "Grandpa, did you know these firefighters?" she asked as she knelt in front of them. "I sure did, Soph," Grandpa replied.

"Look! This one has his picture, a poem and pictures of his family, too," Tyler said as he closely read every word of the remembrance for Michael Esposito. He was

one of Grandpa's closest friends and a captain in the Fire Department of the City of New York (FDNY). "Grandpa, the man right next to him is also a fireman and he has the same last name. Are they related?" Tyler asked. "Yes, they're cousins," replied Grandpa. "Their poor family," Tyler said as he shook his head. Grandpa sighed and nodded.

"Grandma, I see things next to the photos. Like stones with different sayings, or like this butterfly statue and that fisherman statue. Why are these things near the pictures?" Olivia asked. "Members of their family or friends put the items there because they reminded them of the person they lost," Grandma replied.

Like the rest of the family, Sophia was studying the photos one by one, slowly walking through each row. She saw women, men and firefighters. Then she came across an area with members of the City of New York Police Department (NYPD). She knelt down to look more closely at their faces and names. "Our NYPD heroes," she read aloud.

"Look, Tyler," said Grandma. "This is your mom's friend Lori's father." Tyler turned and quickly knelt in front of the remembrance for Harry Taback. "Forever missed. Cherished father, husband and grandfather. All our love for eternity," he read aloud as he took a picture with his phone and texted it to his mother to show her.

Sophia and Grandma sat together on a cement bench to take in a complete view of Angels' Circle. "I can't believe there are so many people here to remember," said Sophia. "Yes, I know," Grandma replied. "Sadly, there are a lot more who lost their lives that day."

Soon, Tyler, Olivia and Grandpa gathered around Sophia and Grandma. The whole family stared at a full view of Angels' Circle. "It's very beautiful," remarked Olivia. "Yes, it is," the family agreed. "Let's pray for all of these people and their families," Grandma said as the family closed their eyes, joined their hands and said a prayer.

"Grandma and Grandpa, you taught us that everyday heroes are regular people who do things that make a difference," Tyler commented. "You said they do what they believe is right without being told and it makes a difference to others. Isn't that exactly what Wendy did?" he asked. "Absolutely. She did, and all the people who helped her make this as special as it is, are everyday heroes, too," said Grandma. "They really are," said Olivia. "This is amazing," added Sophia.

Chapter 3

The next day the family was up by 7 a.m. They had a full day planned and a lot to learn and see. After breakfast, everyone quickly prepared to leave.

"What are we going to see today?" asked Sophia as the family walked to the car. "A lot," said Grandpa. "I think we'll start with a few of the places in New York City."

As Grandpa drove up the street, his cell phone rang loudly through the car's speaker system.

"Hey, Mick," Grandpa answered. "Hey, John, how's it going?" his longtime friend Michael MacDonald replied. "All is well. I am in the car with my wife and grandkids. We're spending the weekend discussing 9/11 and visiting tributes to the fallen," Grandpa said. "Hi, everyone," said Mick. "Hi, Mick," the family replied together.

"Kids, we worked together at FDNY Rescue Companies," Grandpa said. "But on 9/11, Mick was assigned to FDNY's Marine 9 fireboat named the 'Fire Fighter,' which docked in the waters off of Staten Island."

"Oh, cool," said Tyler. "Can you tell us what you remember about September 11th?" "Wow. I wasn't expecting this discussion," Mick chuckled. "But sure, it's my pleasure, Tyler," he continued. "I remember we were ordered to get the fireboat 'Fire Fighter' near the World Trade Center site. We were making our way there and couldn't wait to help. The fireboat, built in 1938, had the most powerful water-pumping abilities of her time, but she wasn't a speed boat, so it was taking longer than we wanted it to."

"Meanwhile, I remember hearing calls for help on the FDNY radio. The calls were coming from a person I actually knew," he continued. "He was trapped in the rubble after the building collapsed." "What did you do?" asked Sophia. "I quickly responded over the radio to inform other people, who might be able to get there faster than we could," Mick said.

"Did they get there to help him?" asked Olivia. "Yes, luckily and miraculously, they got to him and saved his life," replied Mick.

The entire family fell silent as each one thought about

what that must have been like.

"What did you see when you got to the site?" Tyler asked. "I saw a lot of fires burning," Mick replied. "There were fires burning where the buildings collapsed, cars on fire in the streets near the site – about 15 of them. The fire companies on land didn't have water in that area. The fire hydrants they would normally rely on for water weren't working. They were damaged and covered with debris from the collapsed buildings," he continued.

"What did you do?" asked Sophia. "The members of Marine 9 and I set up hose lines. We started pumping as fast as the 'Fire Fighter' could – 20,000 gallons of water a minute – and relaying water from the fireboat to the engine and ladder companies on land that were not buried under the rubble. Marine 9 was pumping and relaying water 24 hours a day for days. For many days it was the only source of water for the north-west area of the site. In addition to making sure the pumps were continuously providing water to put out the fires, members assigned to Marine 9 also helped with the rescue and recovery operation," Mick said.

"That's amazing," said Sophia. "Yeah, it sure was," replied Mick. "I remember the members of Marine 9 and the fire units on land performing extraordinarily well. I was, and

I am still, proud and eternally grateful for the efforts of each and every one of them."

"Mick, I have known you for so many years and I don't think I ever heard that account," Grandma said. "I know it's hard, but we need to make sure these stories are told." "I agree," said Mick. "I am glad you are teaching the kids about that day. You know, kids, you are lucky to have such great grandparents." "We sure are," said Tyler. "Yes, we are," said Olivia and Sophia.

"We have a lot of places we're planning to visit," said Grandpa. "I'll give you a call back tonight, Mick." "10-4," said Mick. "Thank you for sharing that story with us," said Olivia. "Yes, thank you," said Tyler and Sophia. "You're very welcome. Goodbye everyone," said Mick. "Bye," the family replied as the call ended.

"Wow, Grandpa," said Tyler. "I never thought about the fire hydrants not working." "I know," Grandpa replied. "The boats played a critical role in helping with the response, as well as the rescue and recovery operations."

"Do you kids remember when I told you that the subway system was shut down and the bridges and tunnels were closed on September 11th?" asked Grandpa. "Yes," said Tyler, as Olivia and Sophia nodded. "Well Manhattan, the part of New York City we are talking about, is an island. If all the normal ways to get off the island were shut down, how do you think people got away from the area?" he asked.

The kids paused to think. "By boat?" asked Olivia. "Exactly," replied Grandpa. "To get away from the area, hundreds of thousands of people walked south of the World Trade Center site to the water. They had no place to go, but onto boats. When the United States Coast Guard realized this, they made a call on the radio system that boaters use. They asked anyone wanting to help with the evacuation of the people to gather their boats near Governors Island, which is near the southern tip of Manhattan. They didn't know what to expect when they made that call, but within minutes, hundreds responded. Hundreds of boats were on their way, from tug boats, to ferry boats, to party boats and private boats – they all answered the call to help people leave Manhattan," said Grandpa.

"These were regular people who wanted to help in any way they could," said Grandma. "True everyday heroes, who turned up to help. For hours that day, they took people away from Manhattan to safety. They would fill up their boats with people, go across the water to land, unload the passengers, then go back to load more passengers. They did that over and over again for many hours. It wound up being

the largest water evacuation in our nation's history. They had never trained for anything like this. It all happened because everyday heroes answered the call for help."

"That's so unbelievable," said Tyler. Olivia and Sophia agreed.

Chapter 4

Tyler, Olivia and Sophia were shaking their heads in disbelief. "Why haven't we heard these stories before?" Tyler asked. "That's a great question, but let's not focus on why you haven't heard this before. Let's focus on what you are hearing and what else we can tell you to help you learn more," said Grandma.

At that point, Grandpa drove out of the tunnel into the streets of Manhattan. "First, I think we'll show you the FDNY Memorial Wall on the side of FDNY Ten House. That's the firehouse that houses Engine Company 10 and Ladder Company 10 right across from the World Trade Center site. The Memorial Wall is on the outside wall, where all of the passersby can see it and remember the fallen," Grandpa said as he parked the car. The family crossed the street to get to the firehouse.

"Oh, wow!" exclaimed Olivia. "It's beautiful," she said as the family turned to face the wall holding the 56-foot-long, 6-foot-high, bronze sculpture, which is believed to be the largest of its kind in North America.

"Look! Here on the left-hand side is a dedication plaque," Olivia said. "343. This city's bravest. In memory of those who fell and to those who carry on across all cities and towns across all generations. To our fallen friend and partner, volunteer firefighter Glenn J. Winuk," Tyler read out loud.

"On 9/11, Glenn J. Winuk ran from his office to help, but he lost his life that day," Grandma said. "At the bottom of the dedication plaque, that's the name of his company, Holland & Knight LLP and The Holland & Knight Charitable Foundation, which created this memorial to the FDNY," said Grandma.

Tyler read aloud the words inscribed across the bronze panels of art. "Dedicated to those who fell and those who carry on. May we never forget."

"In the center, is that the Twin Towers on fire with clouds of smoke around them?" Olivia asked. "Yes," replied Grandma. "On each side, you can see firefighters responding to the situation and then continuing throughout the recovery operations."

"Whose names are at the bottom?" Sophia asked. "Those are the names of every lost firefighter, engraved into the bronze," Grandma said. "It's so beautiful," said Sophia. "It really is," said Grandpa.

The sidewalk was very busy with people looking at the Memorial Wall. Grandma and Grandpa held hands with Sophia, Olivia and Tyler to gather the family together before crossing the street.

"Next, I want to show you a special place my friend cofounded," said Grandpa as the family walked on the sidewalk. "What does cofounded mean?" asked Sophia. "It means he helped create it with another person," Grandpa said. "My friend's name is Lee A. Ielpi and he is a former FDNY firefighter who lost his son, Jonathan, on 9/11. Jonathan was a firefighter, too." "Grandpa, that's so sad," said Olivia. "It sure is, Liv," Grandpa replied.

As the family walked inside, Grandpa continued. "It was going to take many years to build the National September 11 Memorial & Museum we'll show you later. While that was being developed, we needed a place to remember the people we lost. We also needed a place where people who were affected by that day could explain their experience to others. That's what this is – the 9/11 Tribute Museum."

Olivia pointed to a picture that was part of the wall exhibit. "Grandpa, who is that man in the uniform?" she asked. "That's Lee and he's holding a picture of his son Jonathan," Grandpa replied as the family gazed at the display and began to walk through the museum.

"Why is that metal so twisted?" asked Sophia. "That's a large piece of steel that was taken from the rubble of the World Trade Center. It twisted like that when the building fell," said Grandpa.

The family saw many items saved from the ruins. An FDNY helmet and jacket, equipment, work ID cards, even a child's stuffed lamb. They saw videos from that day and papers people posted in the streets after 9/11 that they hoped would help them find people who were missing. Next, the family closely studied a wall of photos of the fallen and were able to identify by name many of Grandpa and Grandma's friends.

"It's hard to imagine that something so bad could happen that could take them all from us," Tyler commented as he looked at walls of photos. "I know," said Grandma. "That's partly why that day was so shocking and devastating, and why for many of us, it still hurts to talk about it."

As the family began to walk down the stairs, Olivia asked, "What about their families? How did they go on without them?" "That's a great question, Liv," Grandma replied. "It was very hard and it still is. But when you lose someone you love, you never forget them. Instead, you carry them with you in your heart because love never ends. Some families also started charities in the names of their loved ones to help their memory and spirit live on and help others."

Outside, the family held hands as they walked on the sidewalk. "Grandpa, what's that tall building ahead of us?" Tyler asked. "That's One World Trade Center, also known as the Freedom Tower. The Twin Towers used to be the centerpiece of the set of buildings known as the World Trade Center, but today, that building is," replied Grandpa as the family got closer to the site.

"Is that the tallest building in Manhattan?" asked Sophia. "It sure is. In fact, it's the tallest building in the whole western part of the earth. It's 1,776 feet high to symbolize the year of America's independence," said Grandpa.

"Was it built right where the Twin Towers stood?" asked Olivia. "Right near where they stood. Do you see the big, square areas ahead of us?" Grandpa asked. "Yes," the kids replied. "That's exactly where the Twin Towers stood. Those are reflecting pools with man-made waterfalls, which are the biggest in North America," Grandpa explained.

"Why are the pools so big?" Olivia asked. "Each is almost an acre in size. Each represents one of the towers as well as the huge void and absence left when the buildings came down and many people were lost. Through these pools, you can really start to understand how big the buildings were and how much emptiness people felt," replied Grandpa. "Wow, the Twin Towers were huge. So much bigger than I ever imagined," said Olivia.

"What are the names around the pools?" Tyler asked. "Those are the names of all of the people who lost their lives across the areas impacted that day – in New York City, in Shanksville, Pennsylvania and Washington, D.C.," Grandma replied. "At night, light shines through each letter engraved in the bronze," she added.

"Liv's right, the towers were huge, but the loss that day was huge, too. It's easy to see when you are here because all you see is name after name after name of people who lost their lives," said Tyler. "Yes, America suffered great loss," said Grandma.

"Why do some names have white flowers on them?" asked Sophia. "Each day, white flowers are placed near names to mark their birthdays," replied Grandma. "Oh,

Fr[a]cisco Eligio Bourdier   Sebastian Gorki

rtega Campos   Alejandro Castaño   Joni Cesta

rake   Hernando Rafael Salas   Francisco Joseph Tr

wow!" exclaimed Olivia. "It's their birthday today? That means each day different people have flowers next to their names?" she asked. "Yes, that's right, Liv," said Grandma.

"Why are so many people standing around that tree?" Olivia asked as she pointed to her left. "That's known as the Survivor Tree," Grandma responded. "It's a type of pear tree that was severely damaged on 9/11. Its roots were snapped, branches broken and it was found among the rubble. Over several years it was nursed back to life and then returned here. It's a living reminder of survival and resilience, our ability to overcome such a difficult time."

"There's also a museum here we can show you another day. Let's walk back to the car," said Grandpa. He and Grandma reached for the kids' hands to hold them as they walked.

Chapter 5

"Are there more things to see, Grandpa?" Olivia asked. "Yes, now we're going to make our way to the New York City Fire Museum," Grandpa replied.

"What will we see there?" asked Sophia. "You will see a collection of firefighting equipment through the years, including what firefighters used before the trucks we have today were invented. They also have a remembrance to the 343 members of the FDNY we lost that day," Grandpa said as he continued to drive.

"There really are a lot of places to remember 9/11," remarked Tyler. "There are a lot more, too," Grandma said. "Not just here, but all over the country. For example, at the National Flight 93 Memorial in Shanksville, Pennsylvania, there's a 93-foot-tall statue with 40 wind chimes, each representing a person who lost their life there with its own distinct musical note. In Washington, D.C., the National 9/11 Pentagon Memorial recognizes each of the 184 people who lost their lives there with beautiful, engraved benches made of stainless steel and granite. There are many more memorials and tributes across the United States and around the world, too. That should help you put into perspective just how significant that day is in our history."

Just then Grandpa parked in front of what looked like a firehouse. It had red doors and red trim around the windows. "We're here," said Grandpa as the family got out of the car.

As soon as the family walked in the museum, they saw a big horse-drawn steam engine and a tractor-drawn pumper, all equipment used in the old days by firefighters. "Oh, wow! That's so cool," said Tyler, as Olivia and Sophia nodded in agreement. Then the family walked to the right and into the area with the tribute for September 11, 2001.

There was a large display in the center of the room made of black marble with many tiles. Each tile represented one of the 343 members of the FDNY who made the ultimate sacrifice that day. "Every tile has a different face with their name," remarked Olivia. "It also has the American

flag, their badge and which firehouse they worked at."
"Look! The two big spaces in the display look like the Twin Towers, too," said Tyler.

"This tribute remembers the worst day in the history of the FDNY. It's important to remember. We can never forget the sacrifice the 343 members of the department and other people made that day," said Grandpa. "We'll never forget, Grandpa," said Tyler. "No way; we won't," said Olivia. "Nope," Sophia added.

Next, the kids began whispering to each other. Then, staring at each tile, they read aloud together, one by one, every name to honor the heroes.

"That's such a beautiful thing you just did," Grandma said as they finished reading the last name. "I am very proud of you." "Me, too," said Grandpa, "I think it's time for a family hug," he said as the family hugged and Grandma wiped away tears.

Just then, Sophia noticed glass cases along the walls of the room. "Are all of those tools in the cases from September 11th?" she asked as she pointed to them. "Yes, those items were recovered from the ruins, and the many photographs you see are from that day and the days that followed," Grandpa said.

"Look! It's a timeline of that day all along the wall,"

Tyler yelled as he knelt to get a closer look with Olivia and Sophia. "Oh wow! It lists what happened every few minutes," said Olivia as she placed her hand over her mouth in awe. "Look! It says when everything started and it lists the time, too."

"Here it says when the bridges and tunnels were closed, when the airports were shut down, when the last Rescue Company arrived and so much more," said Tyler.

"Wow, this is unbelievable," he continued. "It really is," said Olivia. Sophia agreed as the three studied the timeline for several minutes.

Soon after, the family walked to the car and began their drive back to Staten Island.

"We saw and learned so much today," said Olivia. "We did, but we're not done yet," said Grandpa. "There's one more special place I want you to see on the way home."

"What is it?" Sophia asked. "A September 11 memorial in Staten Island. It honors the people from Staten Island who lost their lives," Grandpa replied. "This time of day we should be able to experience the full effect of the memorial lighting. It is a special sculpture," Grandma added.

"What's a sculpture?" asked Sophia. "It's an object created to represent a person or an idea. The object has height, width and depth, just like objects in the real world.

Statues are examples of sculptures," Grandma replied.

"What person or idea does this sculpture represent?" asked Olivia. "That's a great question, Liv. 'Postcards,' and that's also the name of it. It represents two large postcards that are folded, as if they hold private messages to be shared only between loved ones," Grandma responded.

"Oh, it sounds so special, Grandma," Sophia remarked. "It is, Soph," Grandma continued. "I can't wait for you to see how they are positioned with the water and the view of downtown Manhattan, the area where we just were. Wait until you see how they recognize each person, too."

Grandpa drove into a parking garage and found a spot to park. The family began to walk to the memorial. Soon they made a left-hand turn and were at the top of a set of steps that led to the memorial.

Olivia gasped as she paused on the steps and covered her mouth with both hands.

"Wow, is that it?" asked Sophia as she looked ahead. "It sure is," Grandpa replied. "Let's make our way down the steps so we can take a closer look."

"Whoa! Look across the water!" exclaimed Tyler. "Grandpa, is that the building I think it is?" asked Tyler.

"Yes. That's the Freedom Tower, the area where the Twin Towers stood. It's across the water, located right in the center of 'Postcards,'" said Grandpa.

"Oh, it is so pretty," said Olivia as the family walked between the two large, white pieces of art. "Oh, look! I see names of people and more information about them."

"Look where the light is shining on the side of each name!" yelled Tyler. "Oh, my goodness!" exclaimed Olivia. "I see outlines of their faces!"

"Yes, their profiles are next to each of their names," Grandma replied. "Look! He wears glasses!" remarked Tyler. Sophia's eyes and mouth were wide open. She was stunned. Tyler and Olivia were, too. The kids looked at each person one by one, reading names and facts about them.

"Grandma and Grandpa, it feels like they are here with us," Olivia whispered quietly. "I never imagined it could be this special." "I know. The first time I saw this it took my breath away," Grandma replied. "It's such a personal, thoughtful display."

Tyler walked closer to the water, to look more closely at the Freedom Tower. "What are the names over here?" he asked as he looked at dozens and dozens of names engraved in granite along the water's edge. "Those are people from Staten Island who lost their lives in recent years from 9/11-related illnesses," Grandpa answered.

"What does that mean? What are 9/11-related illnesses?" asked Olivia. "Unfortunately, people developed a number of health issues from that day," Grandpa continued. "You see, when the buildings collapsed, all of the contents in them and the materials they were made of, turned into a dangerous dust. The dust filled the air with large clouds and covered anything it was near. Some people were breathing it in for hours, others for days, weeks and even months, like the first responders. As a result, many people have had many different kinds of health problems through the years."

"Like what kind of problems?" asked Sophia. "Well, our bodies are all different so it affected people differently. In some cases, people had trouble breathing," replied Grandma. "In some, they could breathe but they made a wheezing sound when they did. In other cases, they developed different illnesses that doctors tied to 9/11. Some people have sinus infections all the time. We know people who ran marathons before 9/11 but who had trouble climbing stairs after it. There are many, many different ways people were, and still are, affected by that day."

"That day is still hurting people?" Olivia asked softly.

"It sure is. It hurt people then and it is still hurting people now," said Grandpa. "I didn't know it was possible for one day to have such an effect for such a long time," Tyler commented as he shook his head.

"Grandma and Grandpa," Sophia asked curiously, "do you have 9/11-related illnesses?" Grandma and Grandpa paused as Grandma put her arm around Sophia.

"We do, but we go to our doctors all the time and we will continue to," Grandma replied. "We can tell you a lot more about this another day." The family turned and began to climb the steps to walk back to their car. When they reached the top of the stairs Grandpa said, "I think it's time for another family hug," so everyone smiled and hugged each other.

"I love you so much, Grandma and Grandpa," Olivia said. "Me, too," said Tyler. "And me, too!" yelled Sophia. "Thank you so much for taking us to all the special places we saw," said Olivia. "You taught us so much today," Tyler said. "Yes, we learned so much! Thank you!" exclaimed Sophia.

"I thought it'd be a good idea for us to think and talk about everything we saw," Grandma said. "If we do that tonight and tomorrow, that should help us make sure you understand it all as well as possible."

"That's a great idea," Olivia said. "It really is," said Tyler. "I know! We can start with Angels' Circle and then we can go through each place in the order we saw it!" yelled Sophia. "Can you also show us pictures on the Internet of the memorials in Shanksville, Pennsylvania and Washington, D.C.?" asked Tyler. "Absolutely," replied Grandma.

As the family started to make their way home, Grandpa told the kids how proud he was of them. "I can't wait for you to tell your parents, your cousin Thomas and your friends about everything you are learning," he told them. "I know! I can't wait," said Olivia. "Same here," said Tyler. "They're not going to believe it," added Sophia.

Join Tyler, Olivia and Sophia as they learn more about September 11, 2001 in the *Discovering Heroes*™ series. Visit www.contextproductions.com.

Word List
'9/11 Courage and Tributes'

Devastated

Devastated means feeling shocked or deeply saddened. Countless people felt devastated by what happened on September 11, 2001, and they continue to.

Eternally and Eternity

Eternally means forever and can sometimes refer to appreciation. Eternity means forever or unending time.

10-4

10-4 means OK. It's a code typically used in radio transmissions used by people like firefighters, police officers and boaters.

Evacuation

Evacuation means removal. In this story, people were removed by boat from the land near the World Trade Center site and taken to safer areas.

Passersby

Passersby are people walking past something.

Rubble and Ruins

Pieces of the buildings that collapsed and everything that was in them are called rubble or ruins.

Centerpiece

A centerpiece is a main feature or highlight. Today, One World Trade Center, also known as the Freedom Tower, is the centerpiece of the set of buildings known as the World Trade Center.

Symbolize

Symbolize means a symbol of, or a representation of, something. America gained its independence in the year 1776. The Freedom Tower stands 1,776 feet tall to symbolize America's independence.

Void and Absence

The words void and absence are used to mean completely gone or empty.

Ultimate Sacrifice

The ultimate sacrifice is being willing to do whatever it takes, even to give their own lives, to save others.

Resilience

Resilience is our ability to overcome a difficult time.

First Responder

A first responder is a man or woman who takes action in emergency situations to help and/or rescue people in danger. Firefighters, police and emergency personnel are all examples of first responders.

Real Photos

Grandma and Grandpa thought you would like to see photos of the real people and places mentioned in this book.

Meet Wendy Furtado Pellegrino, the courageous, everyday hero who started Angels' Circle and continues to manage it all these years later.

This is the front of Angels' Circle in the spring.

The décor, flowers and plants in Angels' Circle change to fit with the seasons of the year and the holidays.

Hundreds of people are remembered in Angels' Circle, including one of Grandpa's closest friends, Michael Esposito, his cousin, Frank Esposito and Harry Taback.

The fireboat Fire Fighter has won more awards than any other fireboat in the world. Today, she is a fully functioning boat, memorial and museum called the Fireboat Fire Fighter Museum in Greenport, New York.

The FDNY Memorial Wall is 56 feet long and comprised of fourteen individual bronze panels. At the center, the Twin Towers are shown in flames.

Meet FDNY Firefighter Jonathan Ielpi, who made the ultimate sacrifice on September 11, 2001. Jonathan is the son of Grandpa and Grandma's friend, FDNY Firefighter Lee A. Ielpi, who cofounded the 9/11 Tribute Museum.

Credit: FDNY

43

Today, One World Trade Center, also known as the Freedom Tower, stands at 1,776 feet high as a symbol of America's independence and its strength.

Nearly 3,000 people who lost their lives on September 11, 2001 are remembered at the National September 11 Memorial & Museum. In this picture, you can see the names of the fallen around one of the reflecting pools, with the largest man-made waterfalls in North America.

The New York City Fire Museum is located in what used to be a functioning firehouse built in 1904.

On display in the museum is historic firefighting equipment, like this coal-fired steam engine that was pulled by horses and could pump 700 gallons of water a minute.

Inside the New York City Fire Museum is a special tribute to the 343 members of the FDNY who made the ultimate sacrifice on September 11, 2001. We will never forget.

Between the "Postcards" sculpture on Staten Island, visitors can see the Freedom Tower across the water.

In a touching tribute to the fallen, profiles of the people from Staten Island who lost their lives on September 11, 2001 are part of the "Postcards" sculpture.

Near the "Postcards" sculpture at the water's edge are the names of Staten Islanders who died from 9/11-related illnesses. Since people are still losing their lives, the list of names continues to grow.

The National Flight 93 Memorial in Shanksville, Pennsylvania, is home to this 93-foot-tall statue with 40 wind chimes. Each chime represents a person who lost their life there on September 11, 2001.

The National 9/11 Pentagon Memorial in Washington, D.C. recognizes the 184 people who lost their lives there on September 11, 2001.

About Grandpa

Grandpa is a loving husband, a father to four daughters and a grandfather to four grandchildren. He is a former lieutenant in the Fire Department of the City of New York, where he valiantly served for nearly 25 years. For about 17 of those years, he was assigned to three of the department's five elite rescue units – Rescue 1, Rescue 2 and Rescue 5.

About Grandma

Grandma is a loving wife, a kind, giving and thoughtful mother to four daughters and a grandmother to four grandchildren. She is a former nurse who helped care for countless people throughout her life.

About Tyler, Olivia and Sophia

Tyler is an 11-year-old sixth grader with an infectious spirit and smile who loves America, his family, baseball, football, Fortnite, fishing and being creative.

Olivia is a bright-eyed, determined, 9-year-old third grader who loves an intellectual challenge, art, baking, sports, dance and video on-demand.

Sophia is a witty, playful 6-year-old first grader with a sheepish smile and a sly spirit who loves animals, music, cooking, swimming, gymnastics, mobile devices and video on-demand.

About the Author

Kristie Kiernan Bouryal is an author and an accomplished communications and marketing strategist with more than 25 years of experience building brands, demand and revenue generation across multiple industries. She has a proven track record of success in executive roles spanning global corporate communications, marketing and all forms of media.

Kristie has received numerous awards and recognition throughout her distinguished career, including an International Business Award for Brand Renovation from the Stevie® Awards; Gold Quill Excellence Awards from The International Association of Business Communicators; multiple Gold Hermes Creative Awards from the Association of Marketing and Communication Professionals; the Chairman's Prize for Innovation at The Associated Press; and the news industry's prestigious Peabody Award.

Kristie is a graduate of Syracuse University's S.I. Newhouse School of Public Communications. She is a loving wife, sister, aunt and the oldest of four girls born to a now retired nurse and a former lieutenant in the Fire Department of the City of New York's elite rescue units. Kristie was born and raised in Staten Island, New York and currently resides in New Jersey with her husband.

About the Illustrators

Gabe Ostley was born in Minnesota and graduated from the Savannah College of Art and Design with a B.F.A. degree in Sequential Art. After working in illustration and licensed characters in New York, New York, he moved to Hong Kong where he was artist-in-residence for the Yew Chung Education Foundation. There, his work expanded to include painting, art installation, murals and large-scale sculptures. While still in Hong Kong, his comic book work was published by DC Comics, Devil's Due, and numerous indie publishers and anthologies. Recently, he adapted Declan Greene's play "Moth" into a graphic novel for The Cincinnati Review. In 2018, with his artist wife Haruka, the two formed Gabruka House in Portland, Oregon. Their all ages fantasy graphic novel project, Bokura, is a Portland Regional Arts & Culture Council grant winner.

Haruka Ashida Ostley is a multidisciplinary artist (painter/muralist/mosaic artist/performer) who was born in Japan but grew up living on four different continents with her family. After graduating from Savannah College of Art and Design with a B.F.A. in Painting, she moved to New York City, where she trained at the Stella Adler Studio of Acting. Later, she became an artist-in-residence in Hong Kong before moving back to the USA in 2015. Currently, she works in Portland, Oregon as a freelance artist creating murals, paintings, graphic novels and commissioned portraits.

Haruka enjoys working with people of different backgrounds across different media around the world.

When stories and energies fill her heart, she responds with her brush, color, body, and soul.

www.ru-ostley.com
www.gabrukahouse.com

CPSIA information can be obtained
at www.ICGtesting.com
Printed in the USA
BVHW051510130619
550904BV00001B/1/P